SPORTS ALPHABETS

You'll be on the ball when you make unique personalized gifts using Kristi Bryant's sports alphabets! Use your imagination to finish them with frames or as wall hangings.

LEISURE ARTS, INC. • Maumelle, Arkansas

SOCCER

X	DMC	¼ X	B'ST	COLOR
☆	blanc	☆		white
■	310	■	/	black
e	798	e		blue
	820		/	vy dk blue

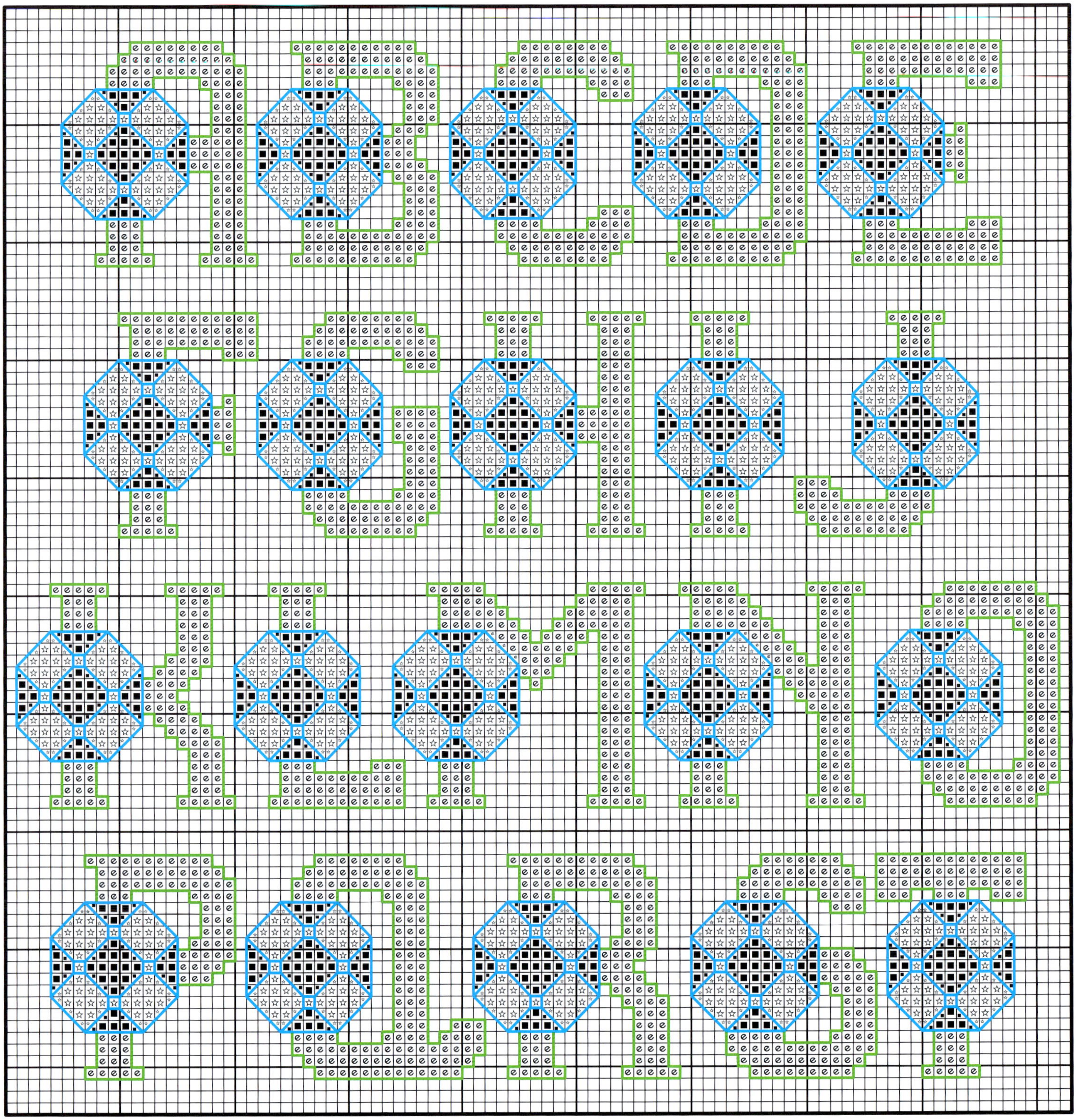

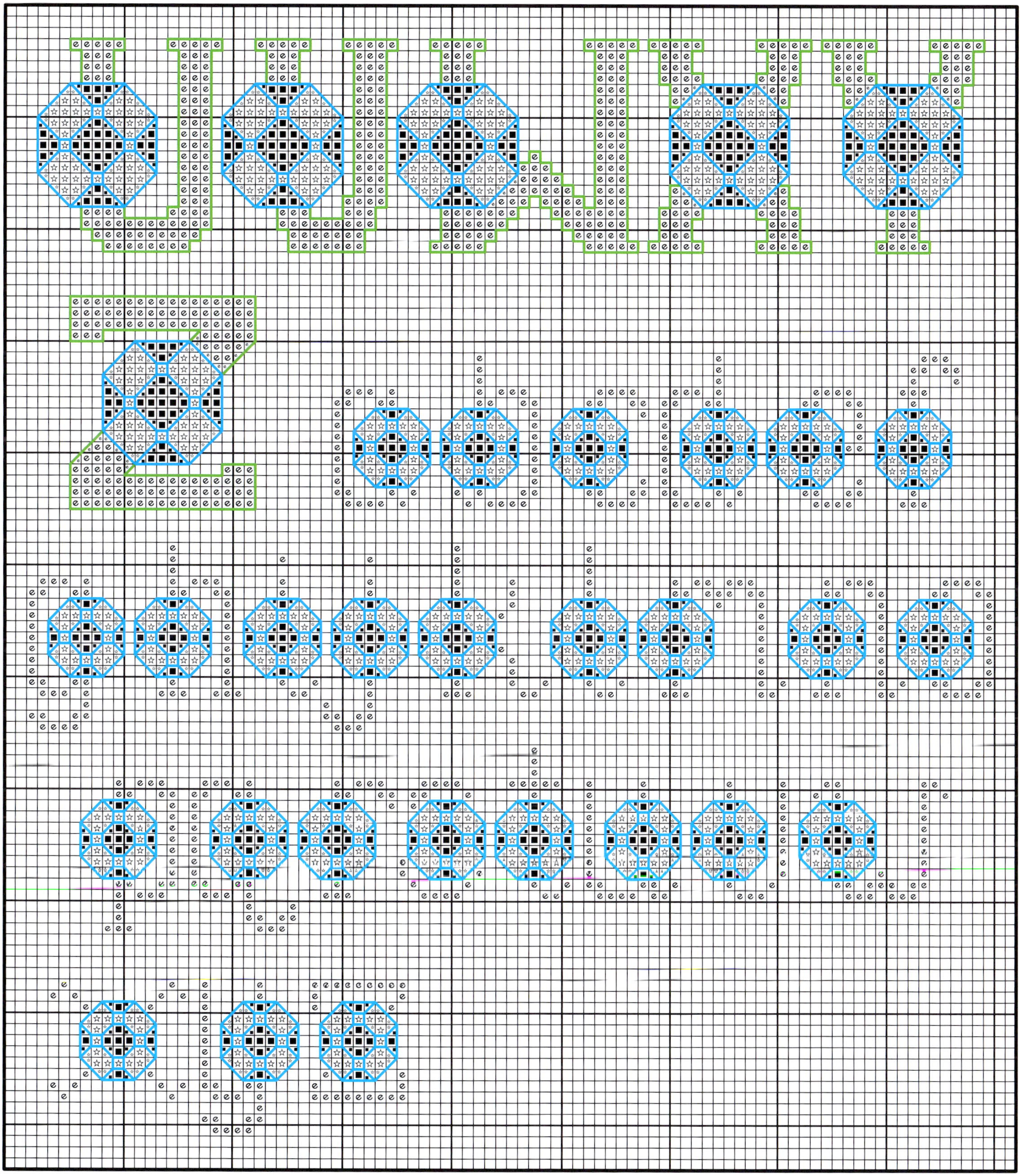

VOLLEYBALL

X	DMC	1/4 X	B'ST	COLOR
☆	blanc	☆		white
	310		blue line	black
	3844		red line *	dk turquoise
8	3846	8		turquoise
● *	3844			dk turquoise Fr. Knot

*Use 2 strands of floss.

BOWLING

X	DMC	1/4 X	B'ST	COLOR
☆	blanc			white
■	310	◪	/	black
¢	720	◪¢	/*	orange
●*	720			orange Fr. Knot

*Use 2 strands of floss.

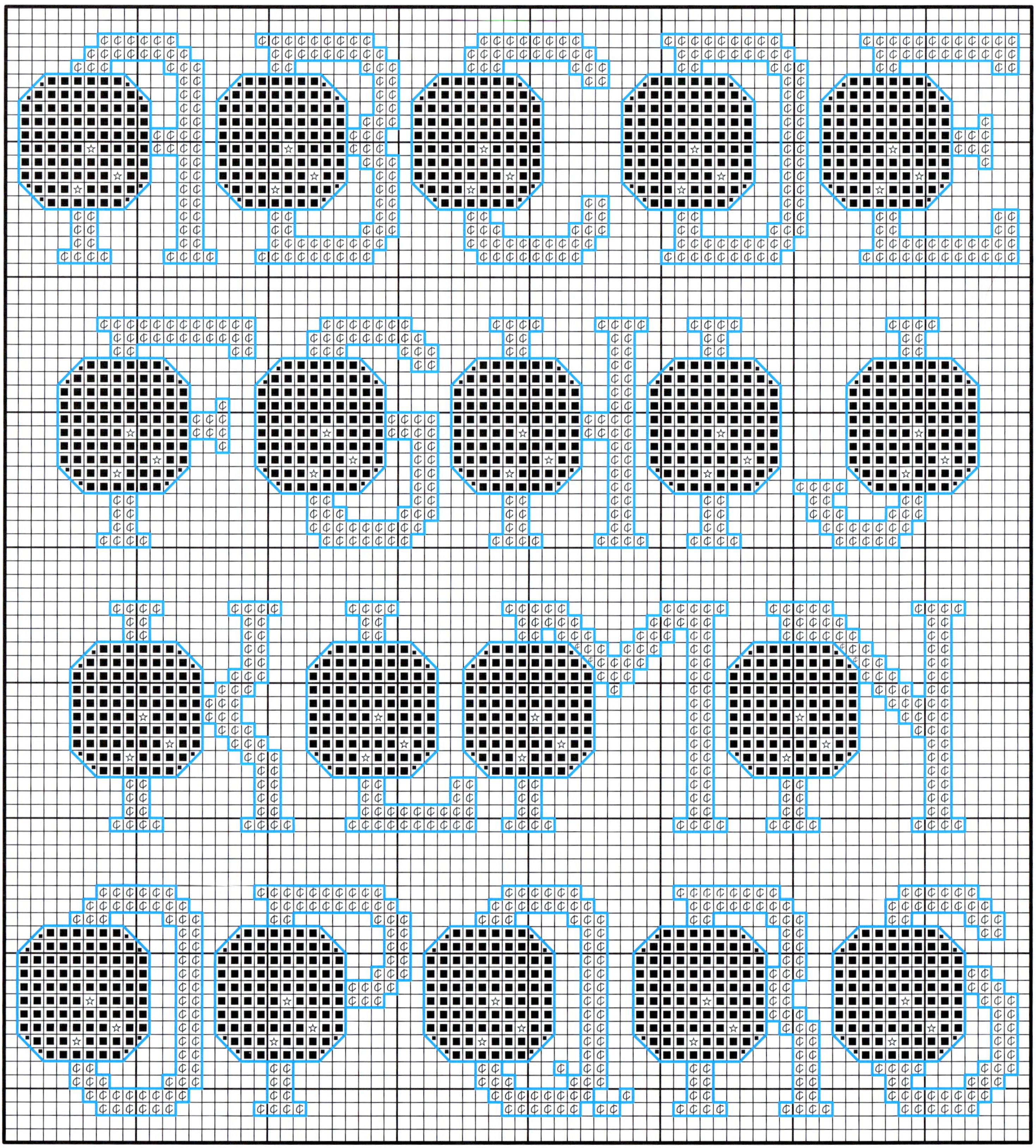

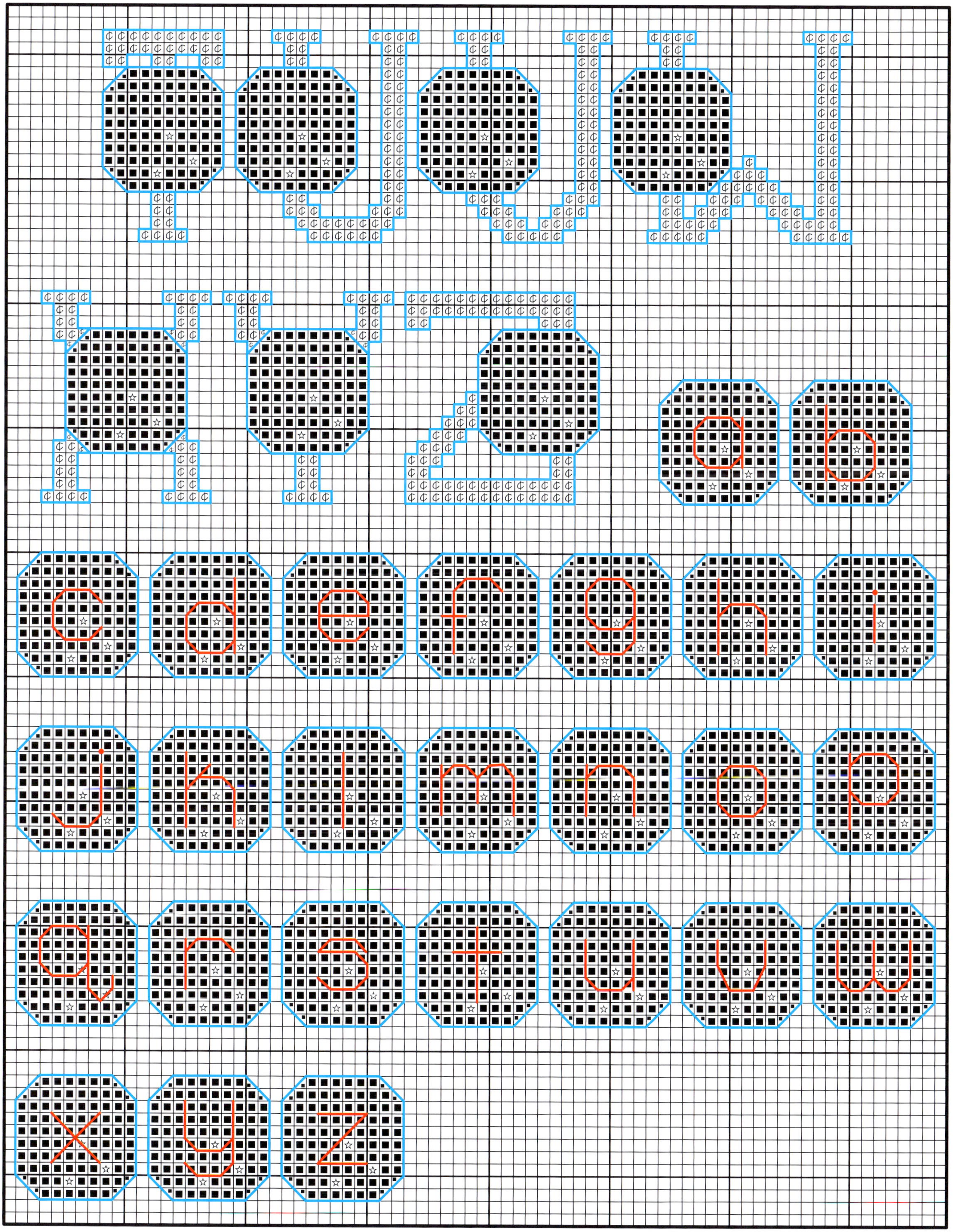

GOLF

X	DMC	1/4 X	B'ST	COLOR
☆	blanc	☆		white
◒	318	◒		lt grey
	413		/	grey
🡅	415	🡅		vy lt grey
m	702	m		green

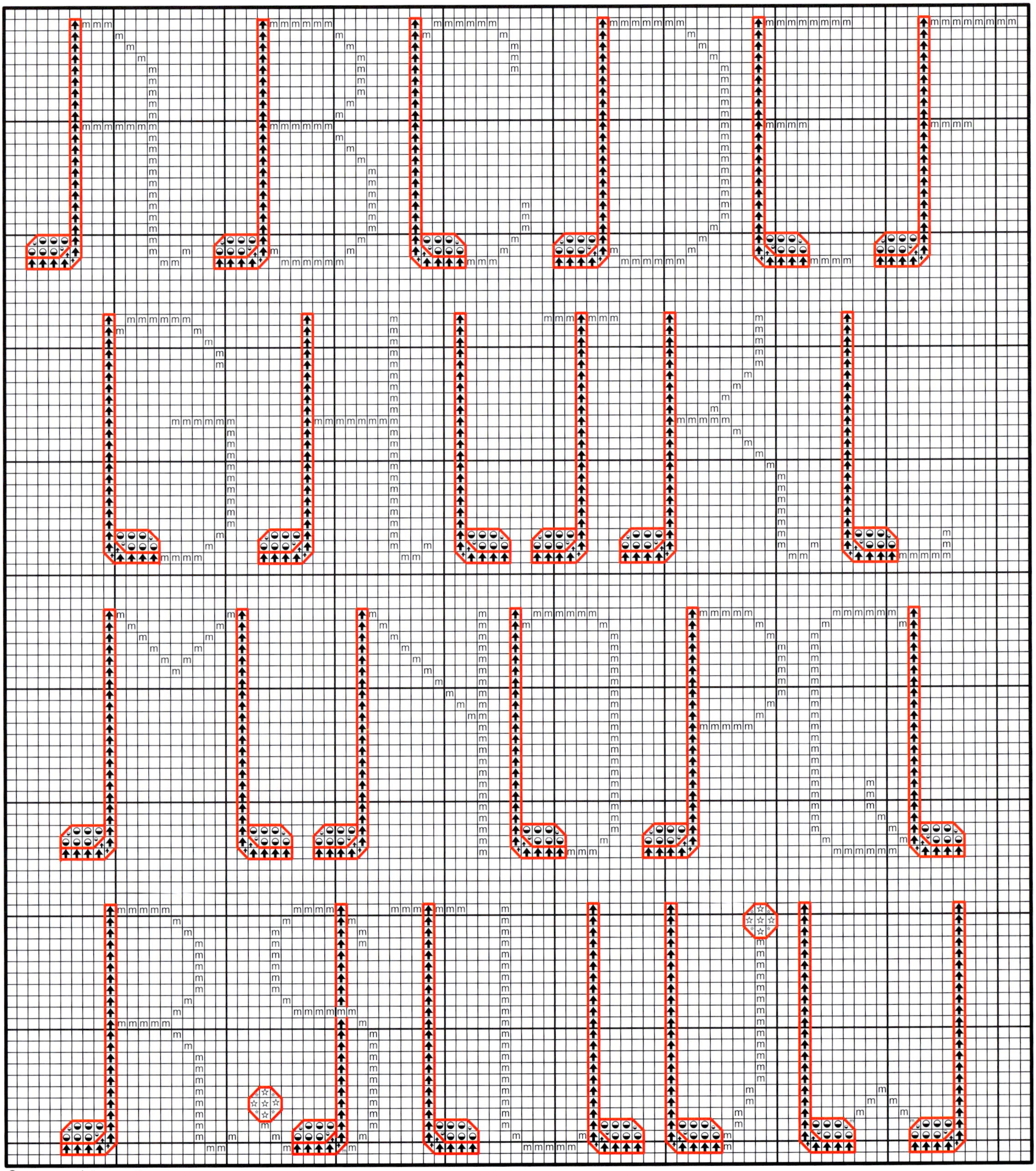

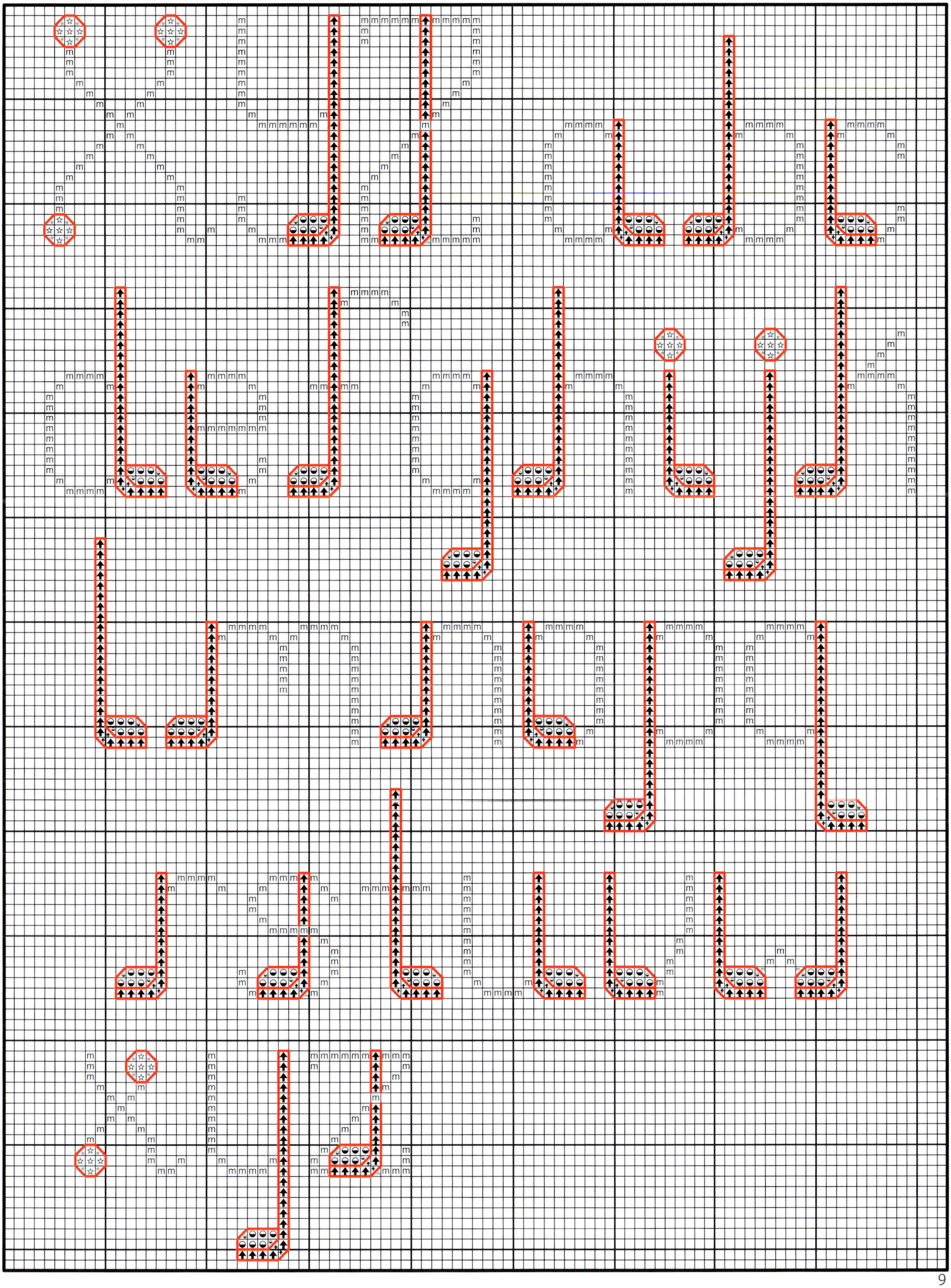

BASEBALL

X	DMC	1/4 X	B'ST	COLOR
☆	blanc	☆		white
	321		/	red
#	433	#		brown
3	435	3		dk tan
⧓	3325	⧓		blue
	3371		/	dk brown

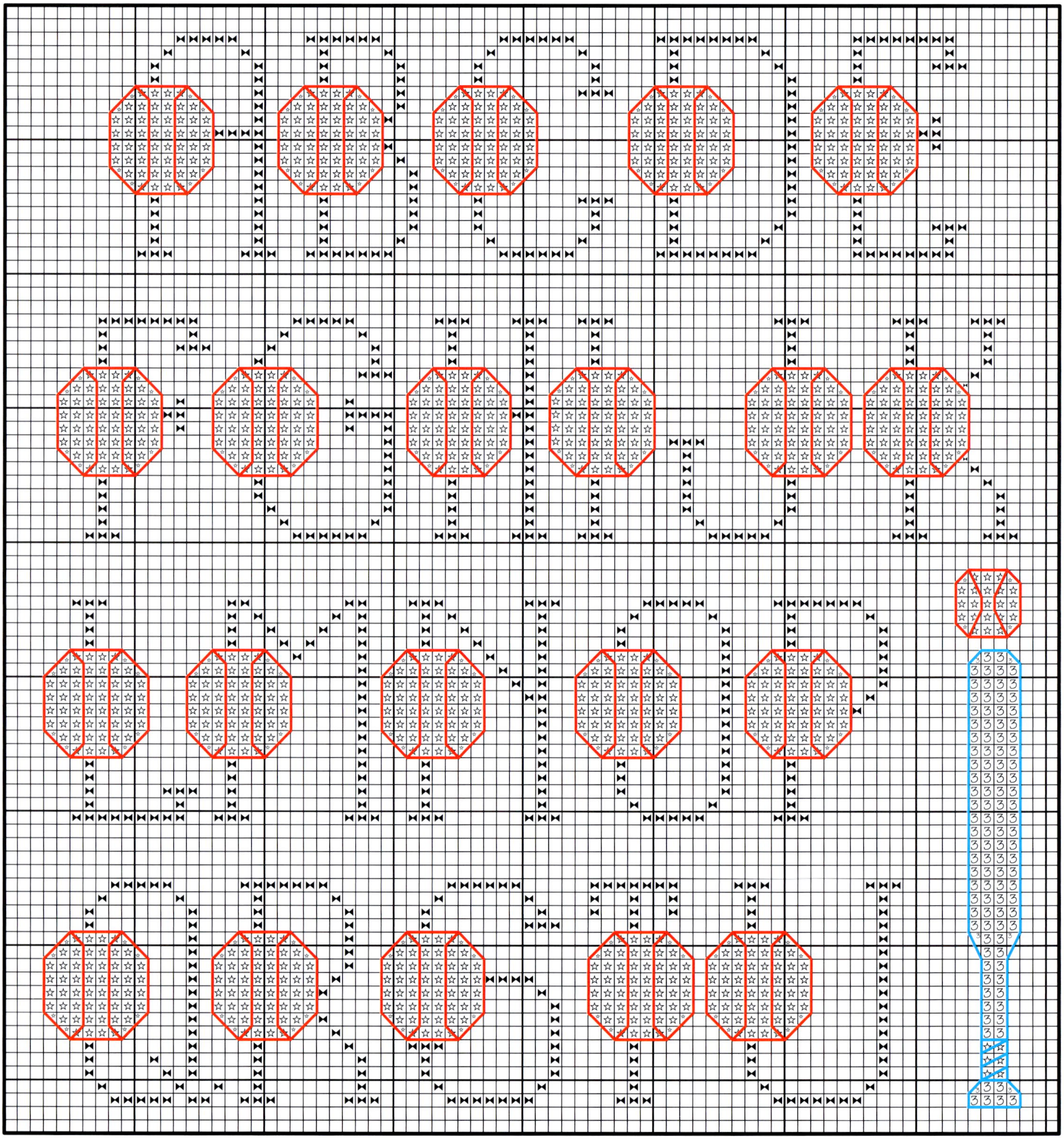

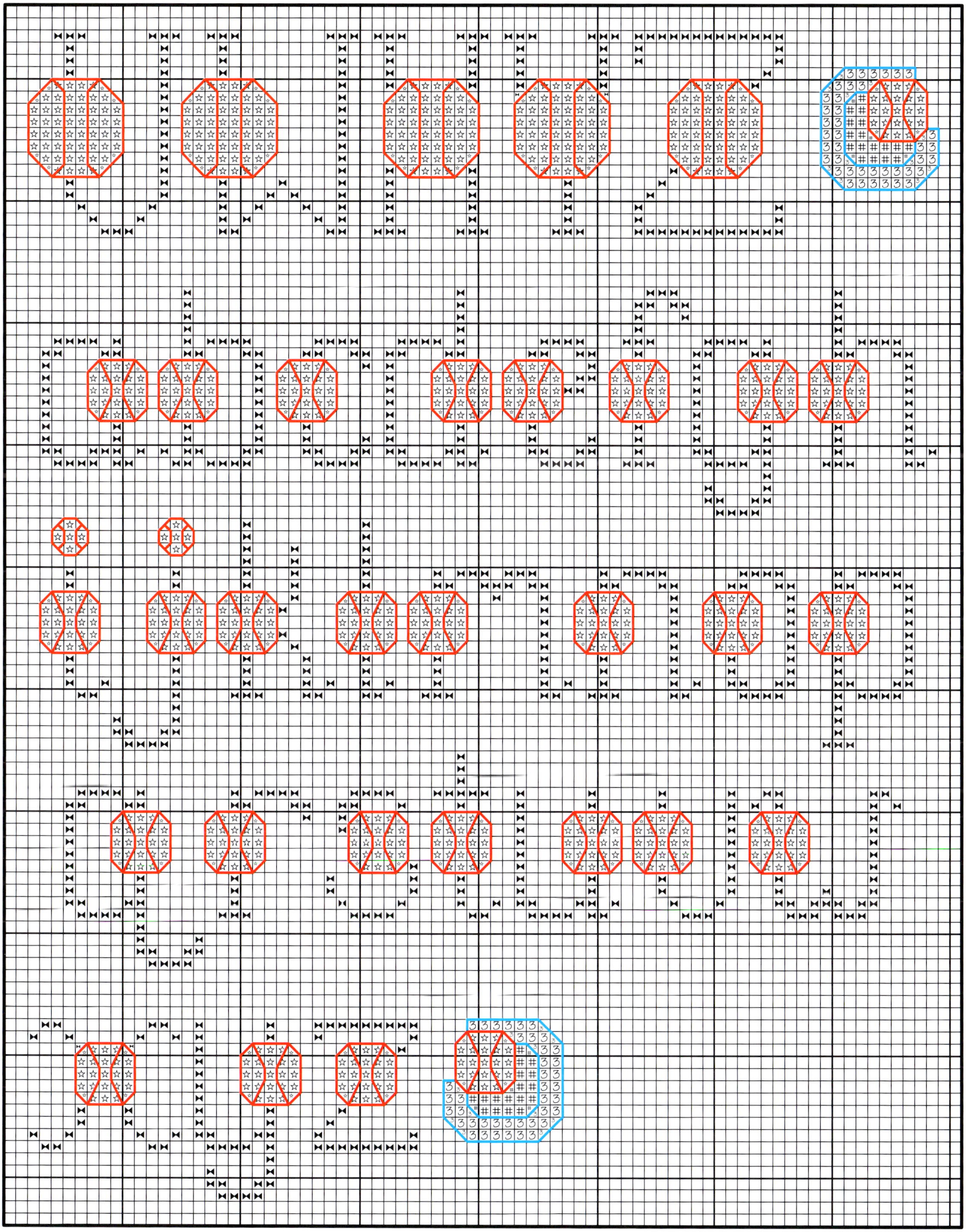

BOUNCY BALL

X	DMC	¼ X	B'ST	COLOR
☆	blanc	☆		white
7	211	7		lavender
	333		/*	purple
	956		/	dk pink
▲	957	▲		pink
●*	333			purple Fr. Knot

*Use 2 strands of floss for lowercase letters.

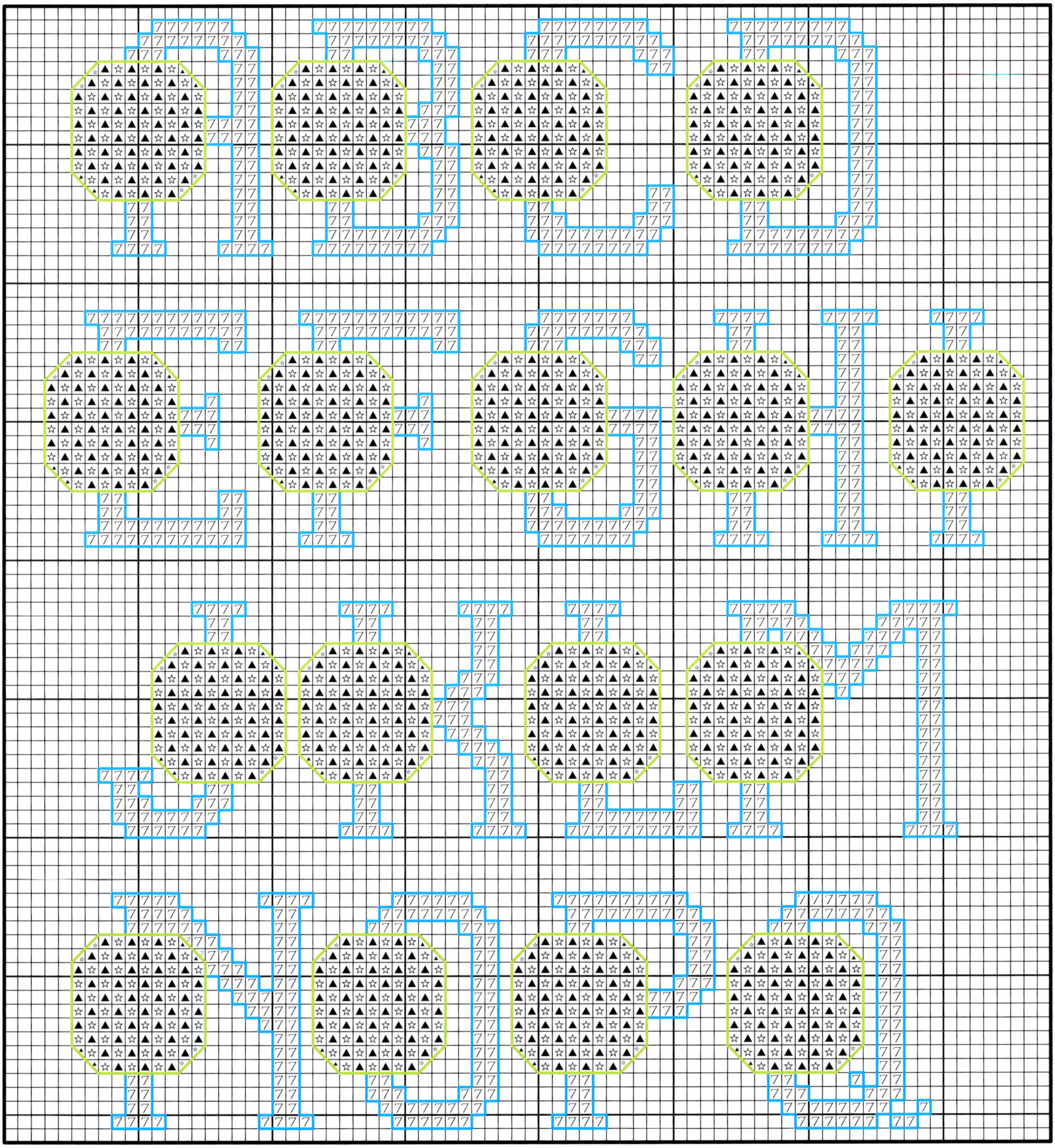

TENNIS

X	DMC	1/4 X	B'ST	COLOR
☆	blanc		/*	white
)	436	)		tan
◇	444	◇		yellow
●	912	●		green
	938		/	dk brown

*Use 4 strands of floss.

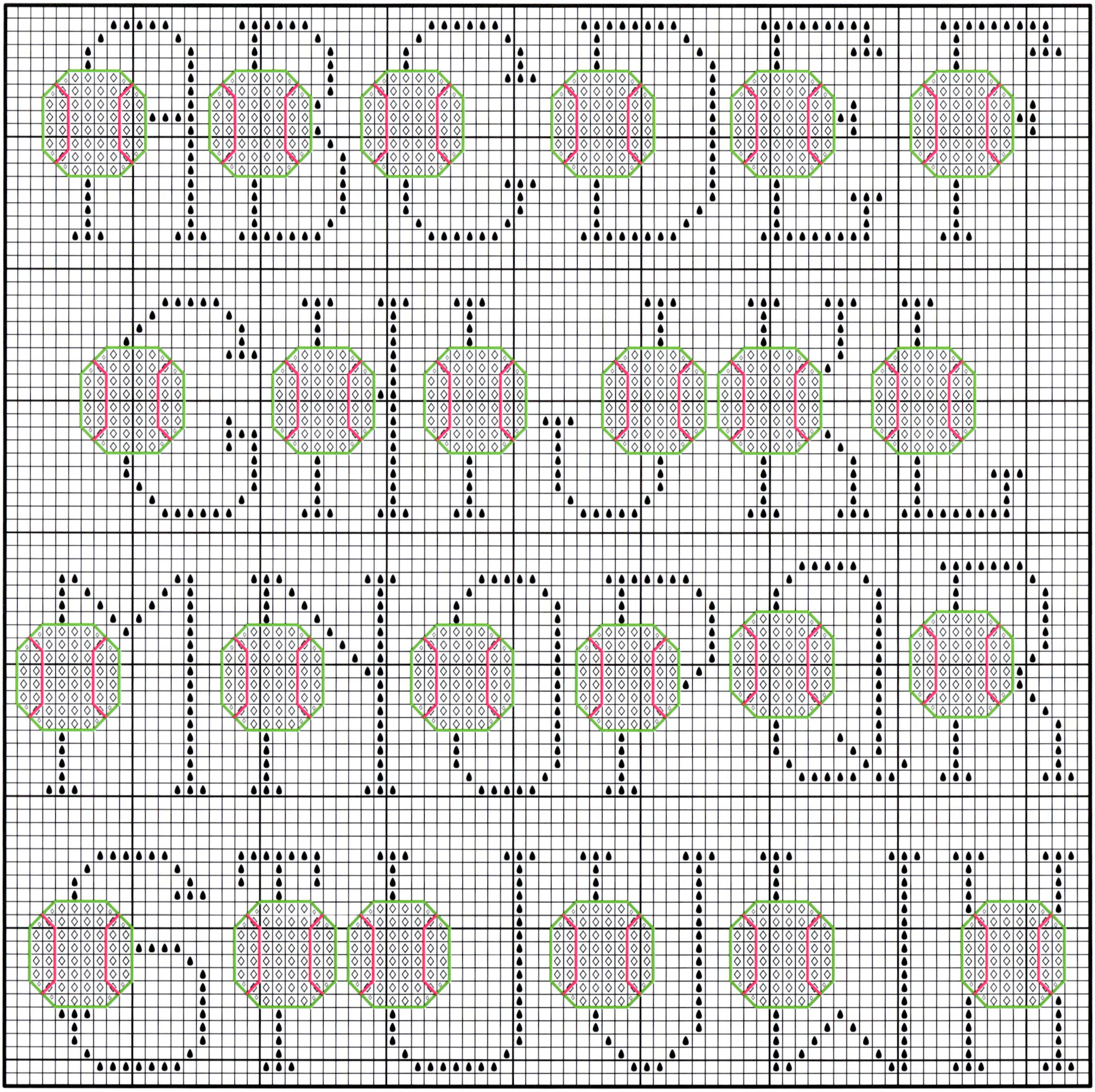

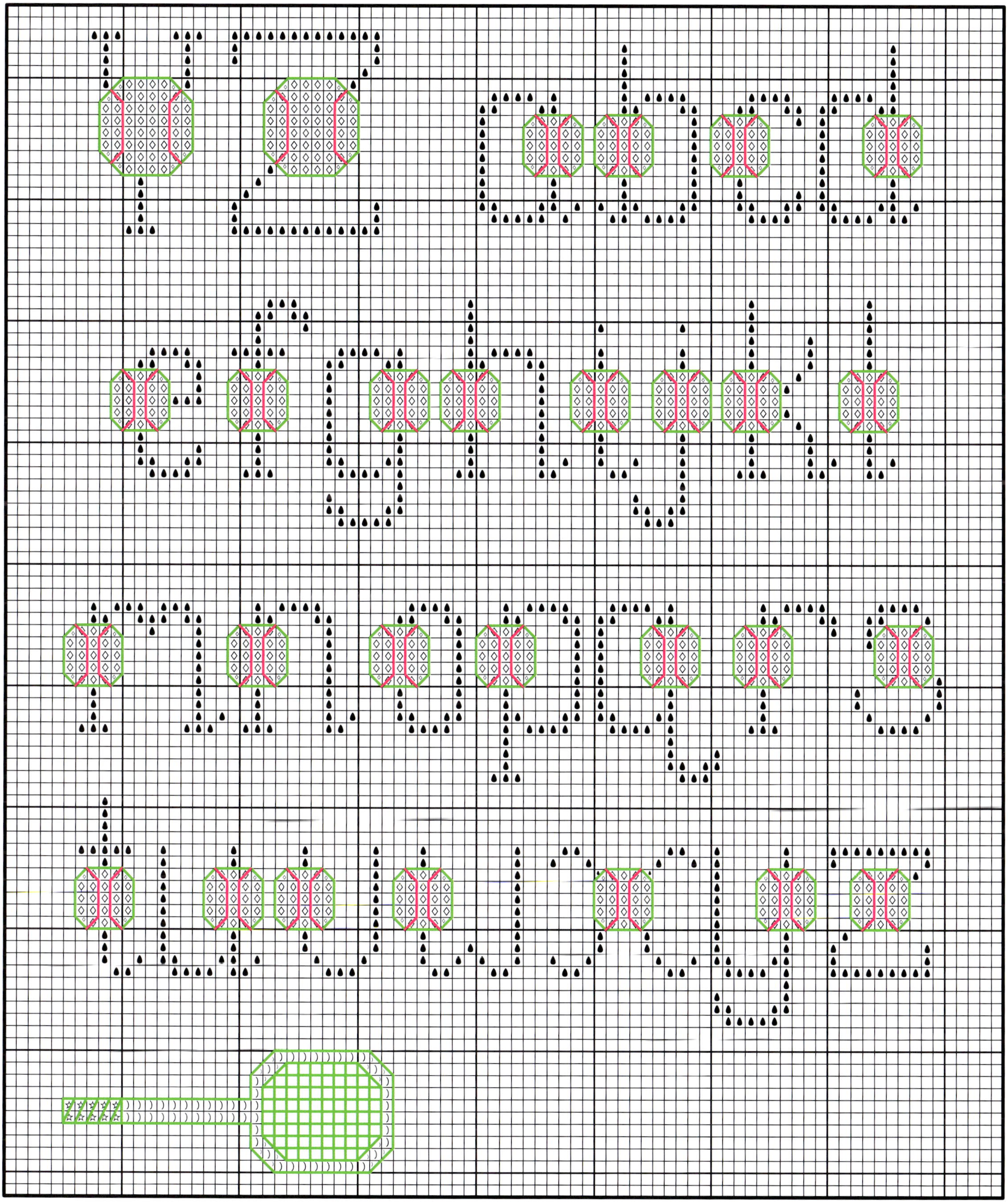

BASKETBALL

X	DMC	1/4 X	B'ST	COLOR
	310		/	black
+	721	+		orange
✓	796	✓		blue

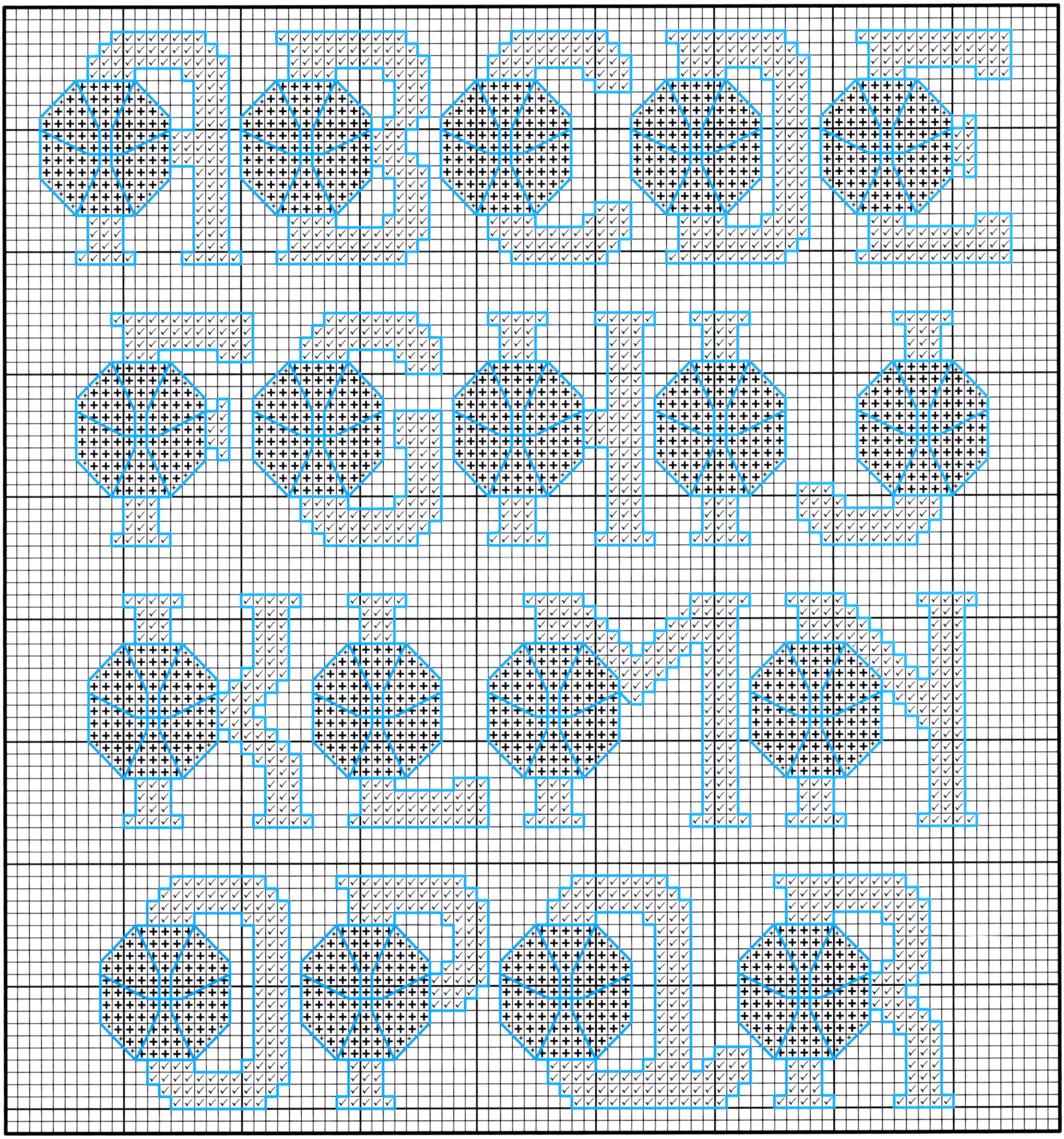

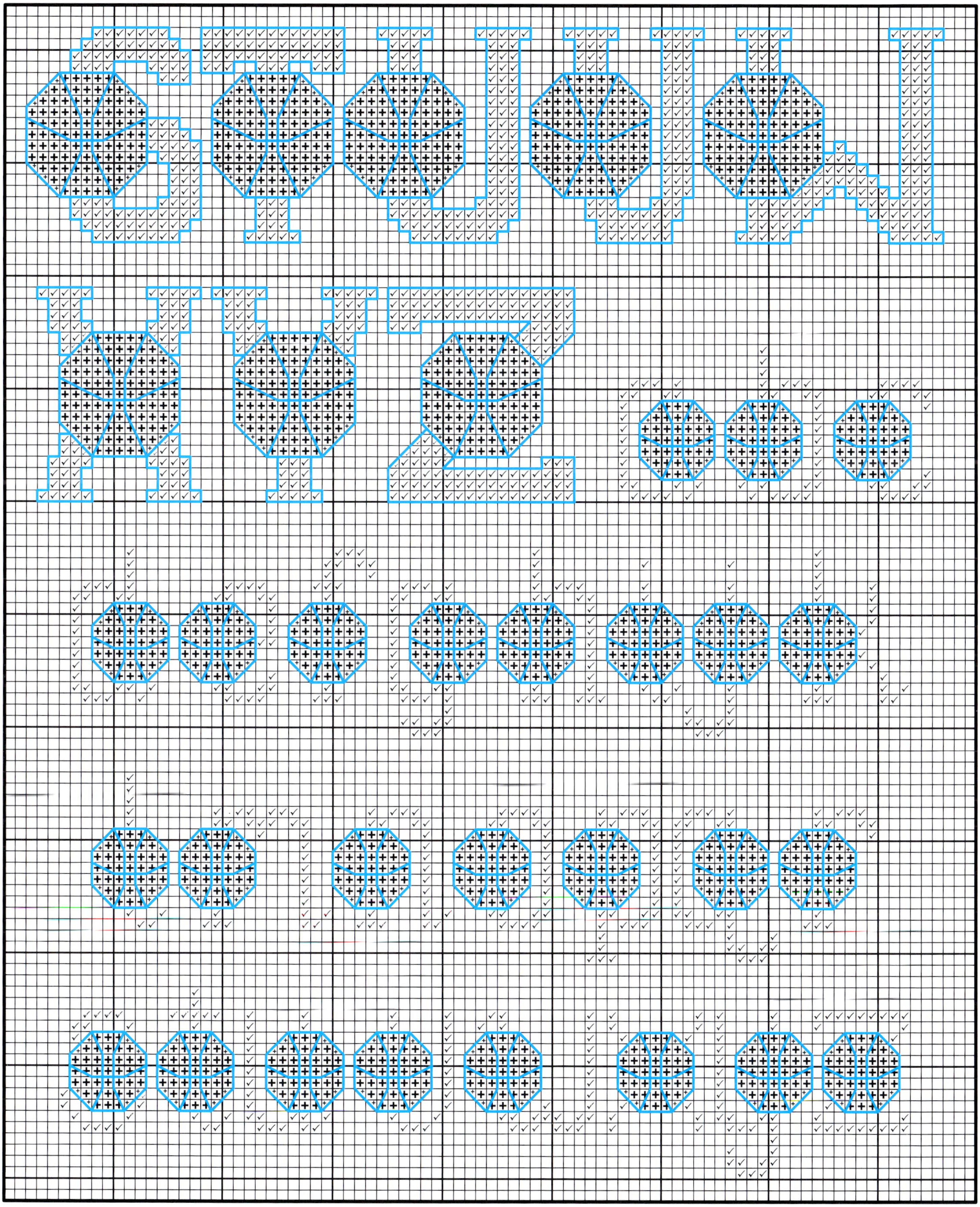

HOCKEY

X	DMC	B'ST	COLOR
■	310	/	black
#	433		brown

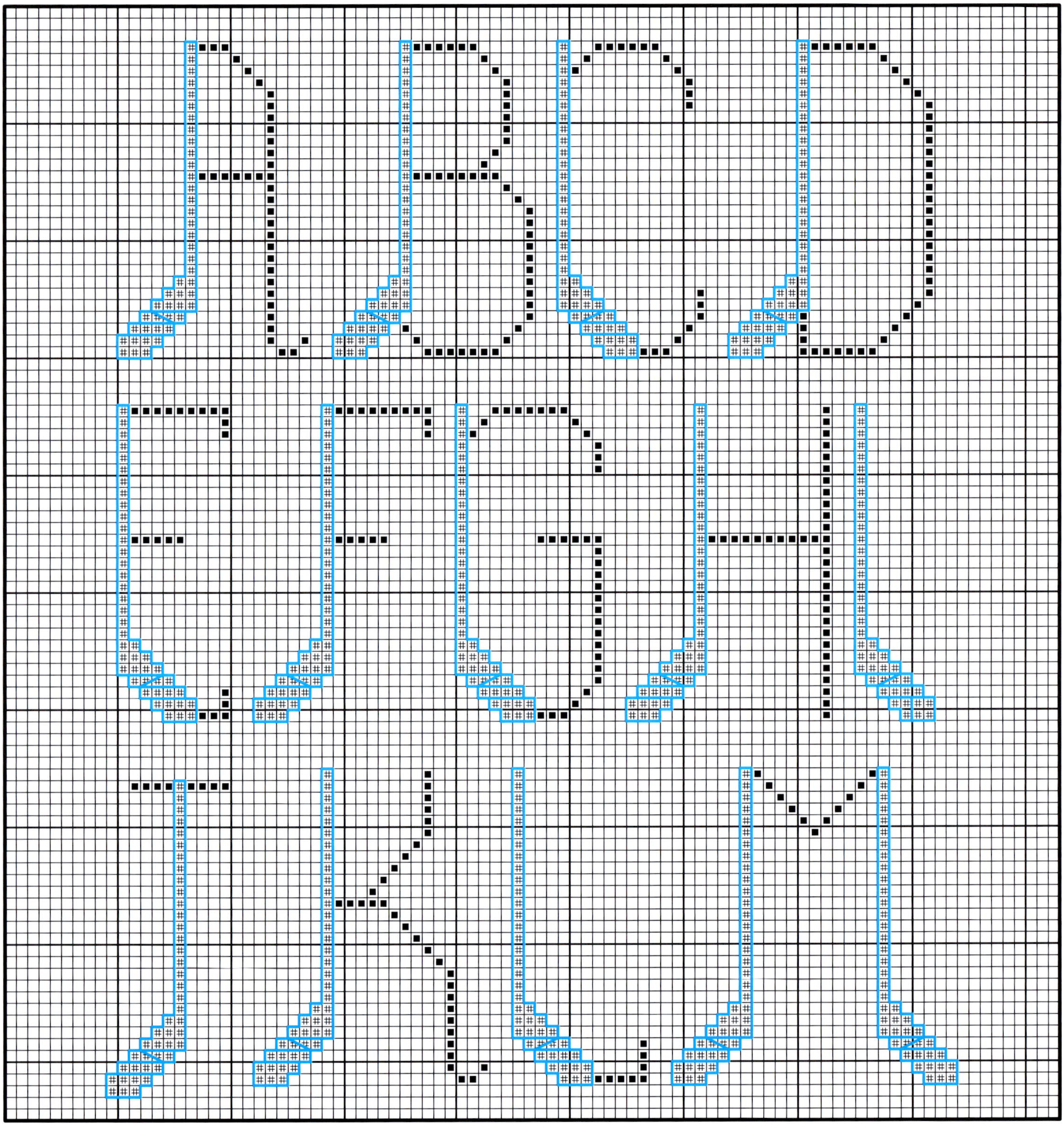

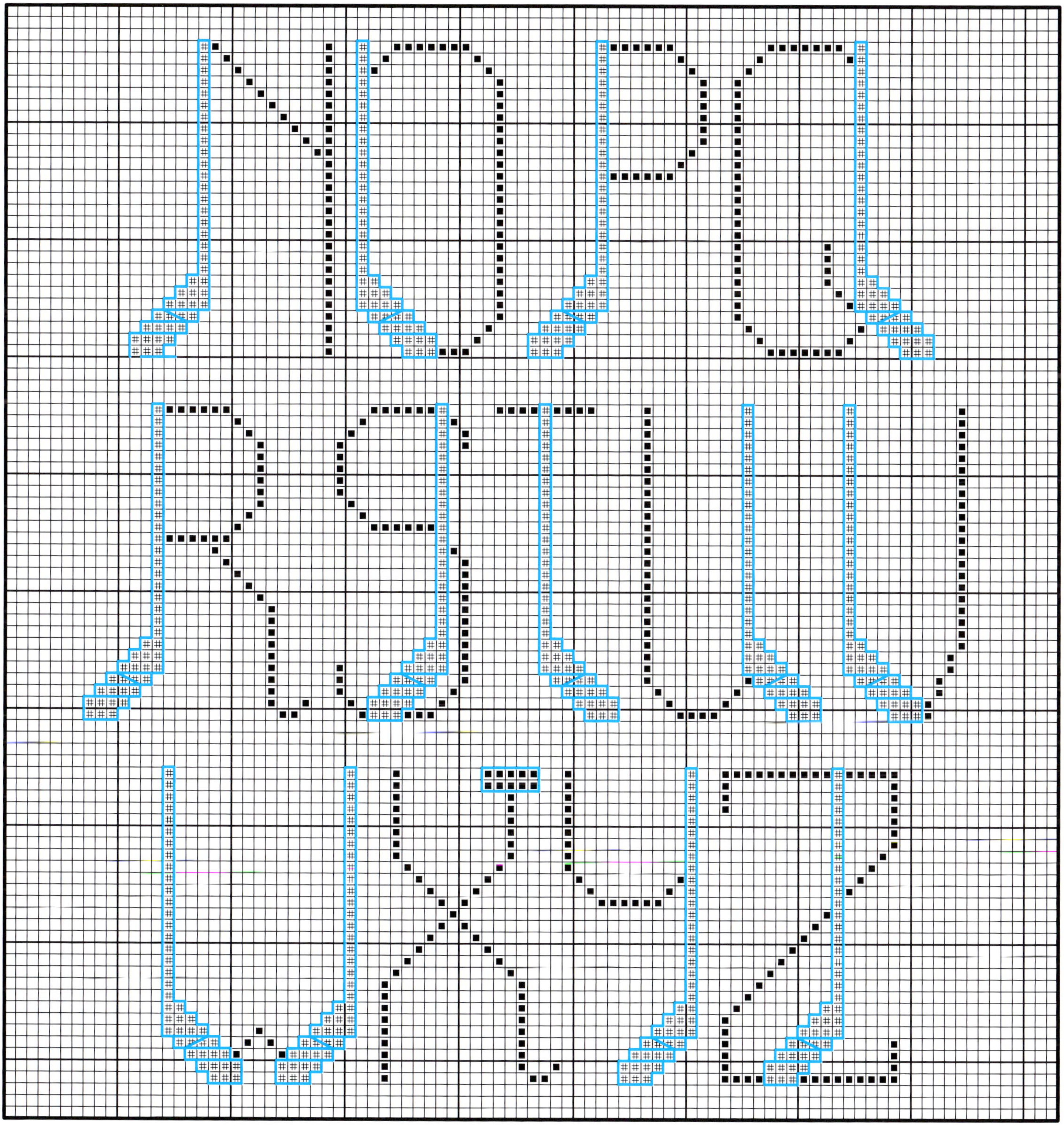

Hockey continued on page 20.

HOCKEY *Continued*

X	DMC	B'ST	COLOR
■	310	/	black
#	433		brown

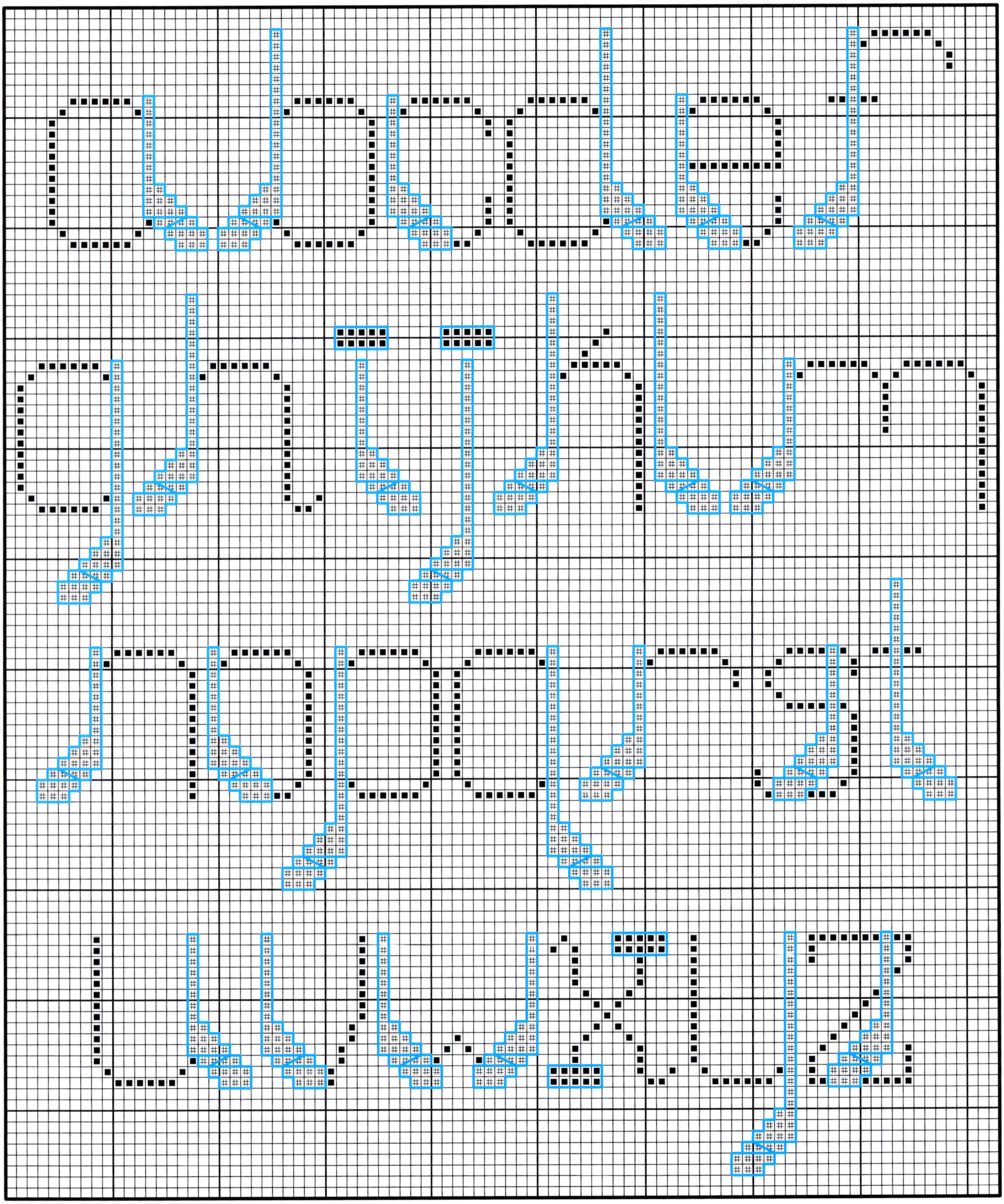

FOOTBALL

X	DMC	1/4 X	B'ST	COLOR
	blanc		/*	white
	310		/	black
▼	321	◺▼		red
#	433	◺#		brown

*Use 2 strands of floss.

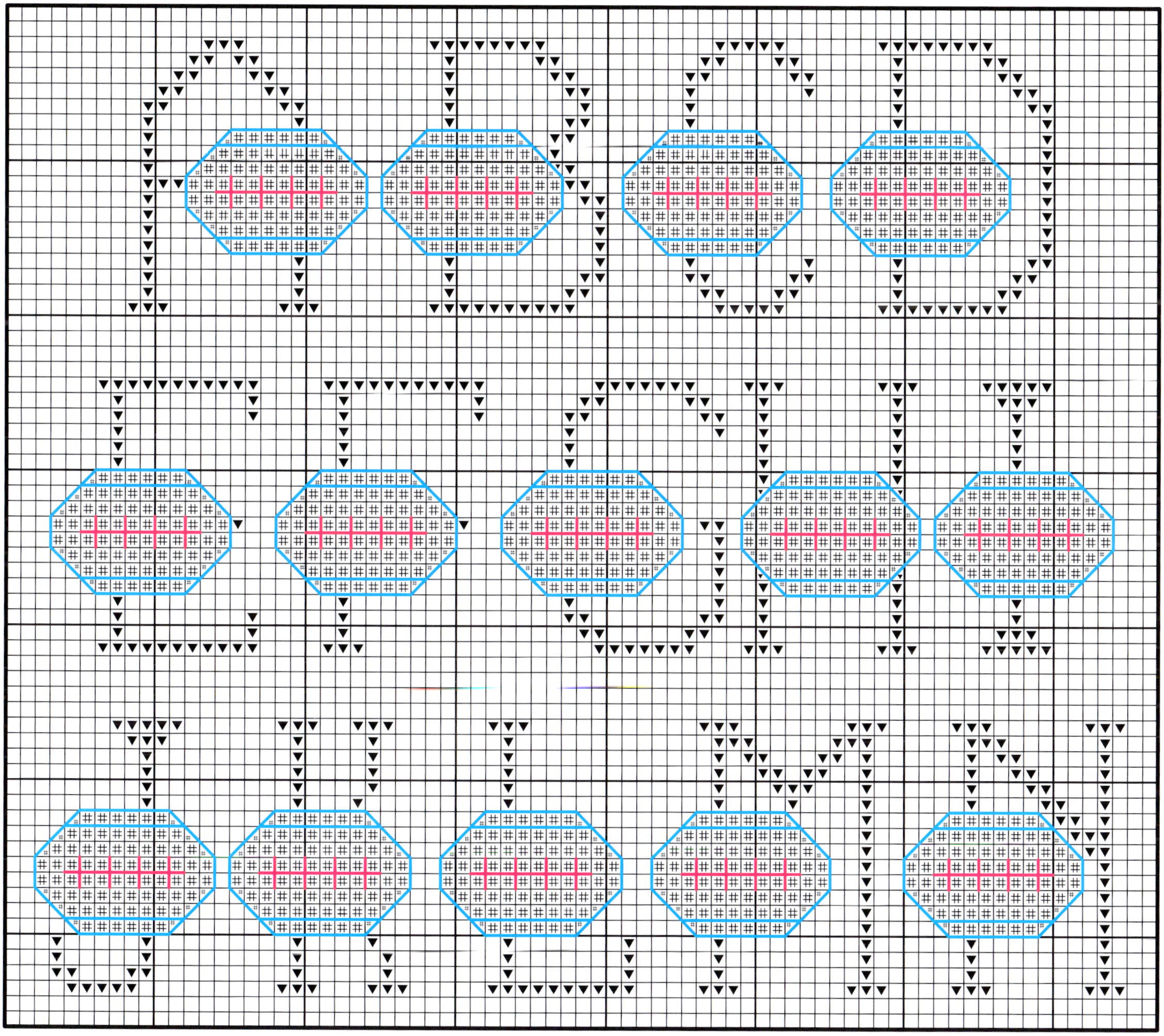

Football continued on page 22.

FOOTBALL

Continued

X	DMC	1/4 X	B'ST	COLOR
☆	blanc		⁄*	white
	310		⁄	black
a	317	◺a		dk grey
◒	318	◺◒		grey
▼	321	◺▼		red
#	433	◺#		brown
▷	desired team color #1			
♥	desired team color #2			

*Use 2 strands of floss.

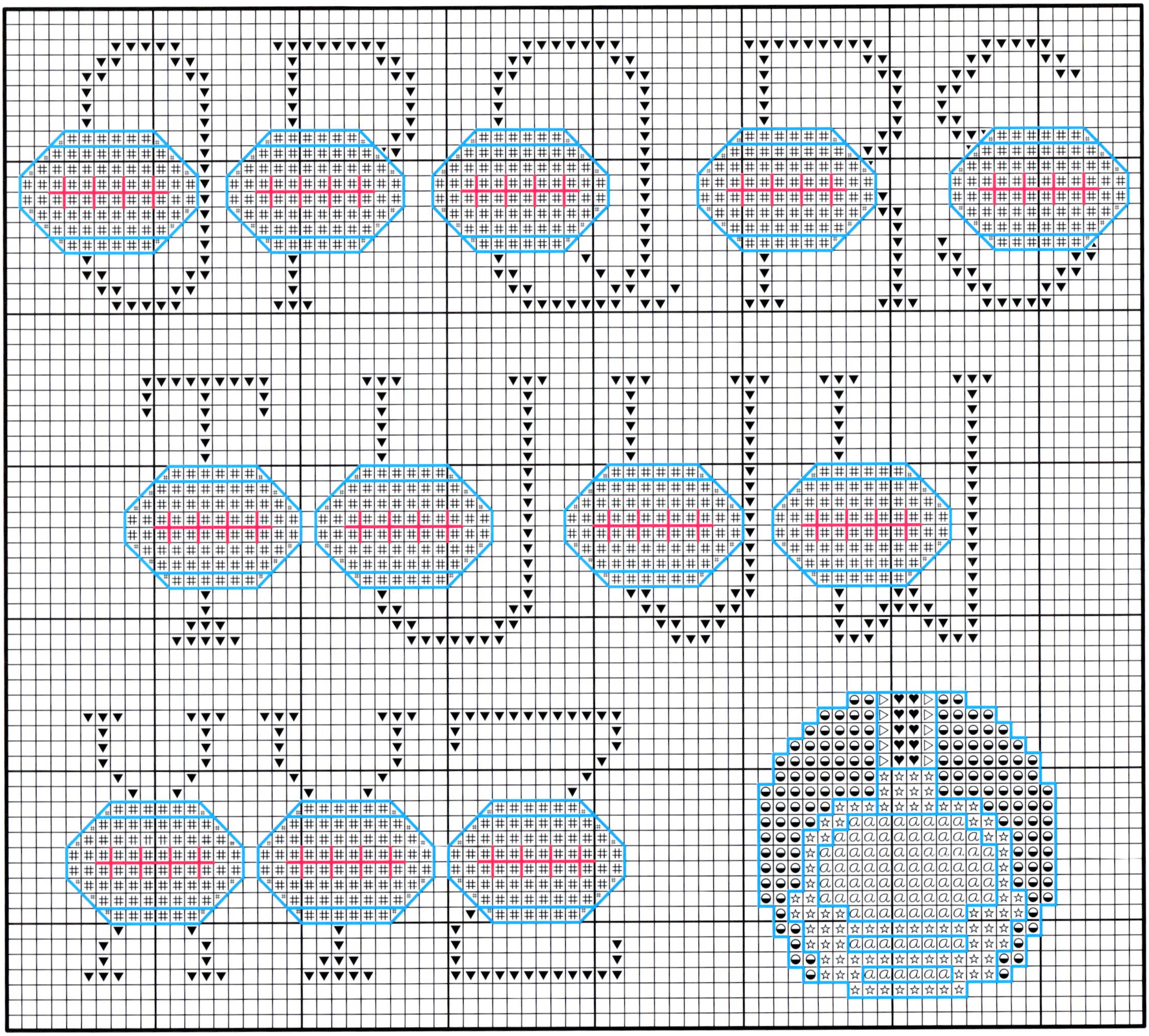

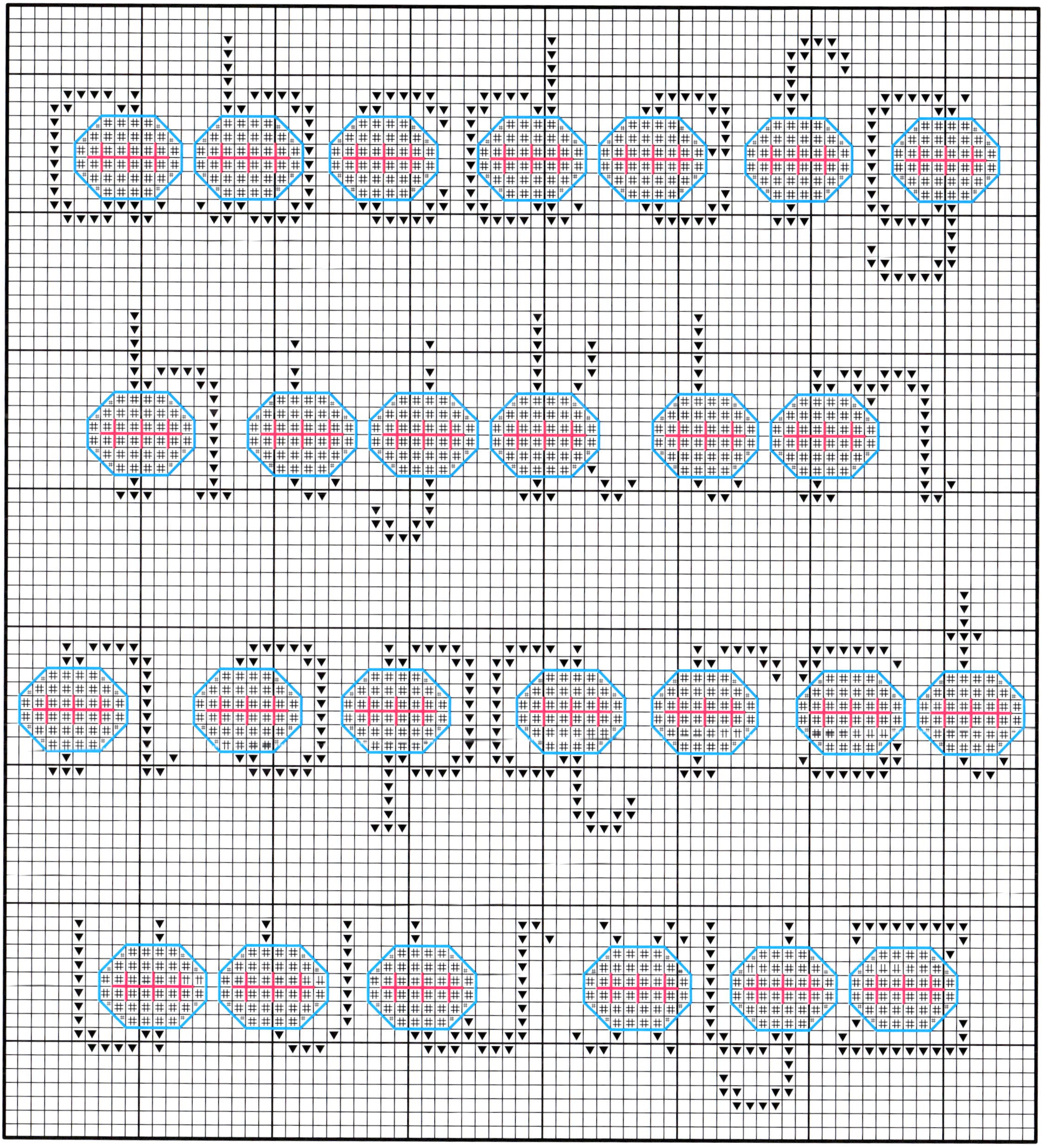

FOOTBALL STAR

X	DMC	1/4 X	B'ST	COLOR
☆	blanc		/*	white
	310		/	black
@	317			dk grey
◒	318			grey
#	433	◿		brown
▷				desired team color #1
♥			/*	desired team color #2

*Use 2 strands of floss and long stitches.

Grey area indicates last row of previous section of design.

Design was stitched on a 15" x 13½" piece of 14 count white Aida (design size 8⅝" x 7¼"). Two strands of floss were used for Cross Stitch and 1 strand of floss for Backstitch and French Knots, unless otherwise indicated. It was personalized with the alphabet on page 28 and placed in an 8" x 10" frame.

Stitch Count (120w x 100h)

14 count	8⅝" x 7¼"
16 count	7½" x 6¼"
18 count	6¾" x 5⅝"
22 count	5½" x 4⅝"

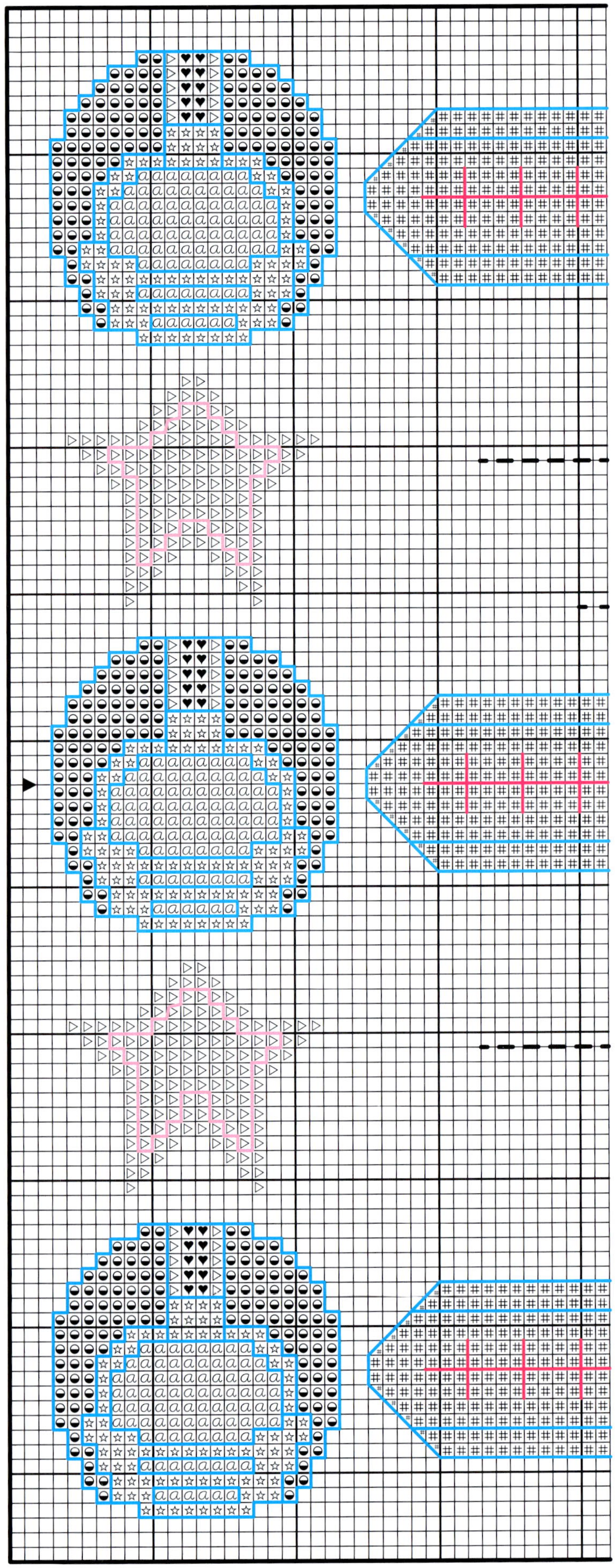

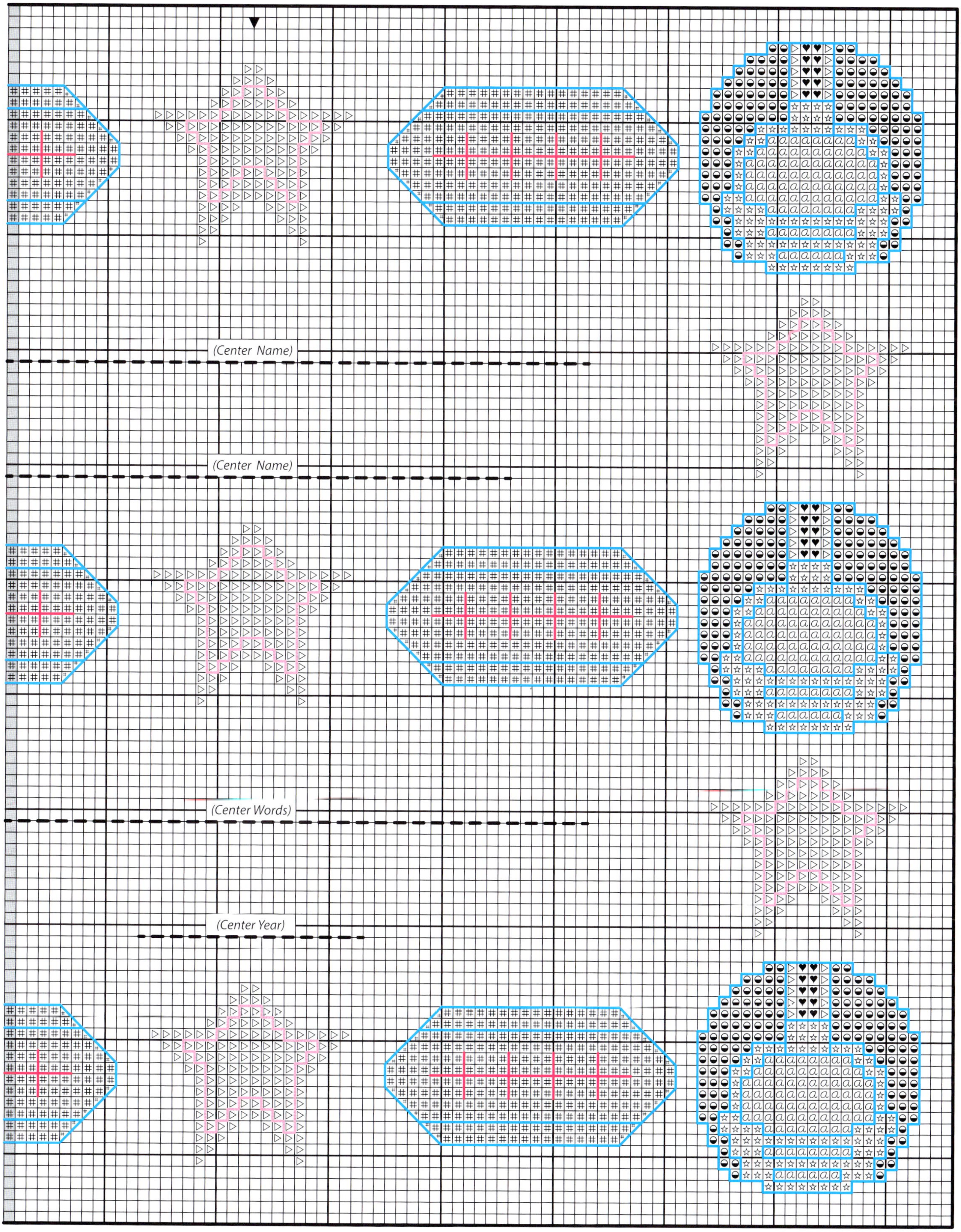
(Center Name)
(Center Name)
(Center Words)
(Center Year)

BIRTH ANNOUNCEMENT

X	DMC	1/4 X	B'ST	COLOR
☆	blanc	☆	/ *	white
■	310	■	/	black
◒	318	◒		lt grey
	321		/	red
	413		/	dk grey
∩	414	∩		grey
#	433	#		brown
3	435	3		dk tan
)	436	)		tan
+	721	+		orange
	3371		/	dk brown

*Use 2 strands of floss.

Grey area indicates last row of previous section of design.

Design was stitched on a 15" x 12½" piece of 14 count white Aida (design size 8⅝" x 6¼"). Two strands of floss were used for Cross Stitch and 1 strand of floss for Backstitch and French Knots, unless otherwise indicated. It was personalized using the alphabet on page 28 and made into a wall hanging with 3" wide sports-themed fabric borders.

Stitch Count (120w x 87h)

14 count	8⅝" x 6¼"
16 count	7½" x 5½"
18 count	6¾" x 4⅞"
22 count	5½" x 4"

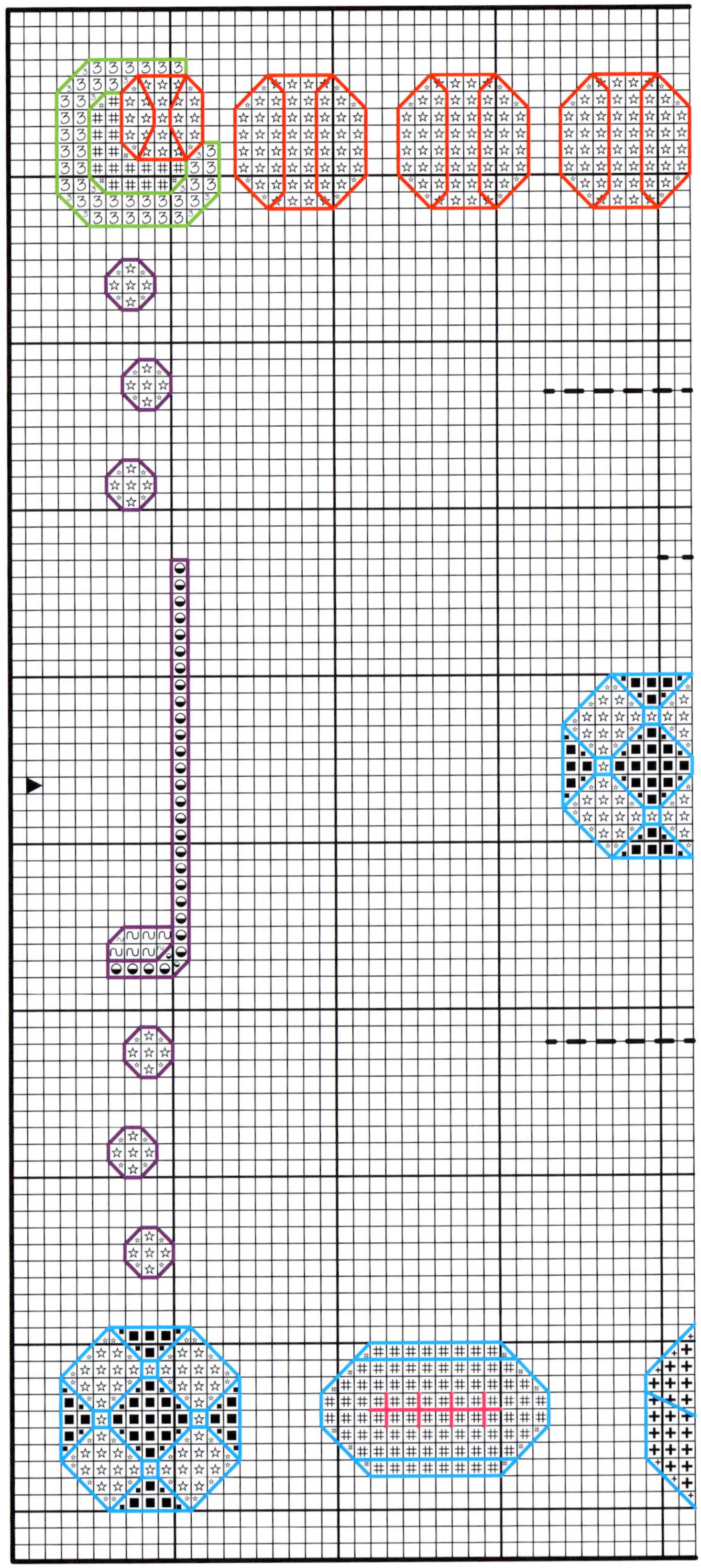

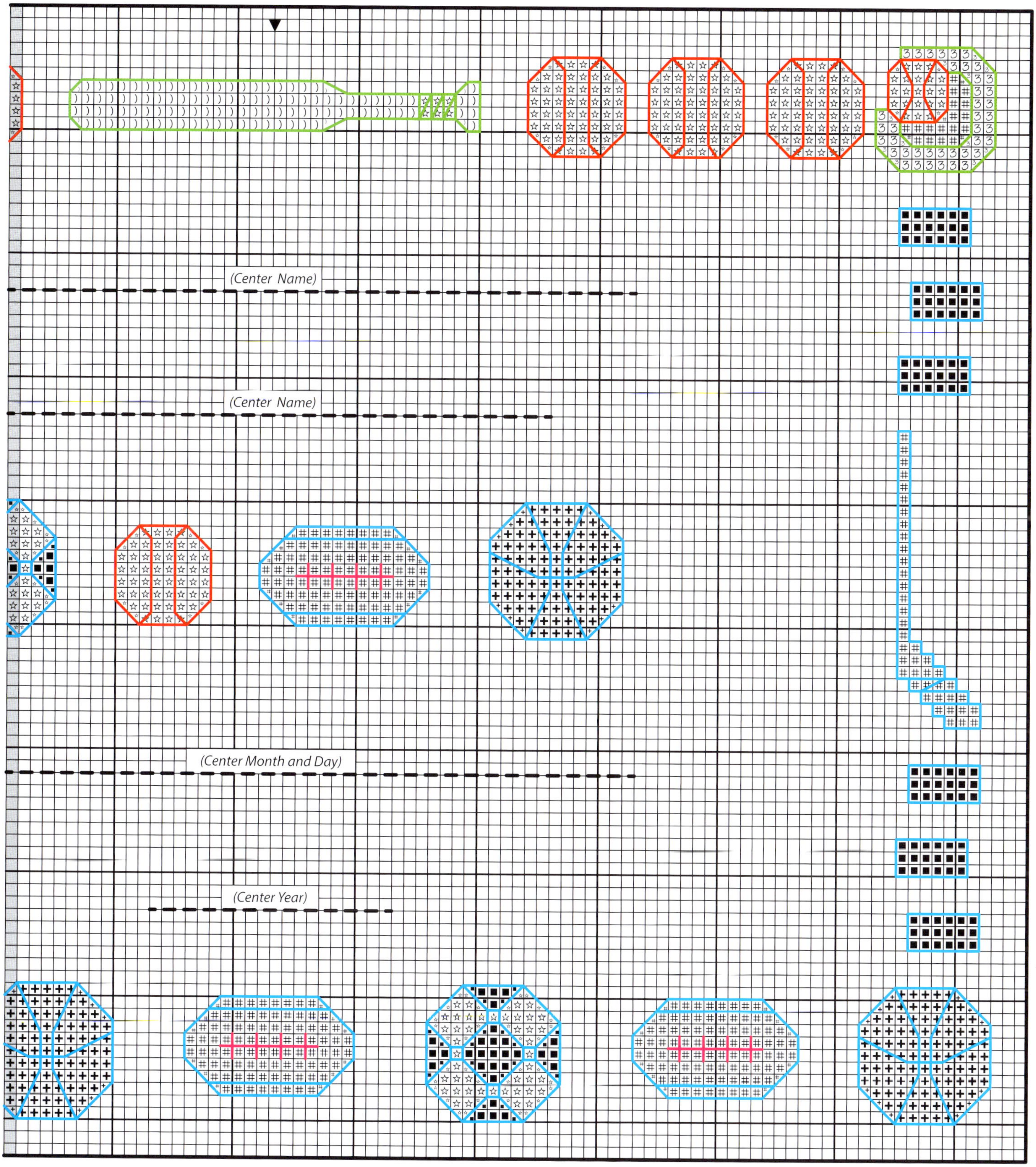
(Center Name)
(Center Name)
(Center Month and Day)
(Center Year)

PERSONALIZATION

These 10 sports-themed alphabets are extremely versatile. Each alphabet has both upper- and lowercase letters, as well as motifs and accessories that can be isolated and used. There are hockey pucks and sticks, baseballs, gloves, and bats, tennis balls and racquets, helmets and footballs and more. Stitch the star in any color to highlight your sports super star. Turn the motifs to the left, the right, or top to bottom–use them to create one-of-a-kind, personalized gifts for friends and family! We've created a Football Star design and a Multi-Sports Birth Announcement (charts on pages 24-27), as well as shown you how you can combine balls and accessories with the letters to stitch a unique name plate (right). Be sure to read the General Instructions, beginning on page 31, to get started designing and stitching.

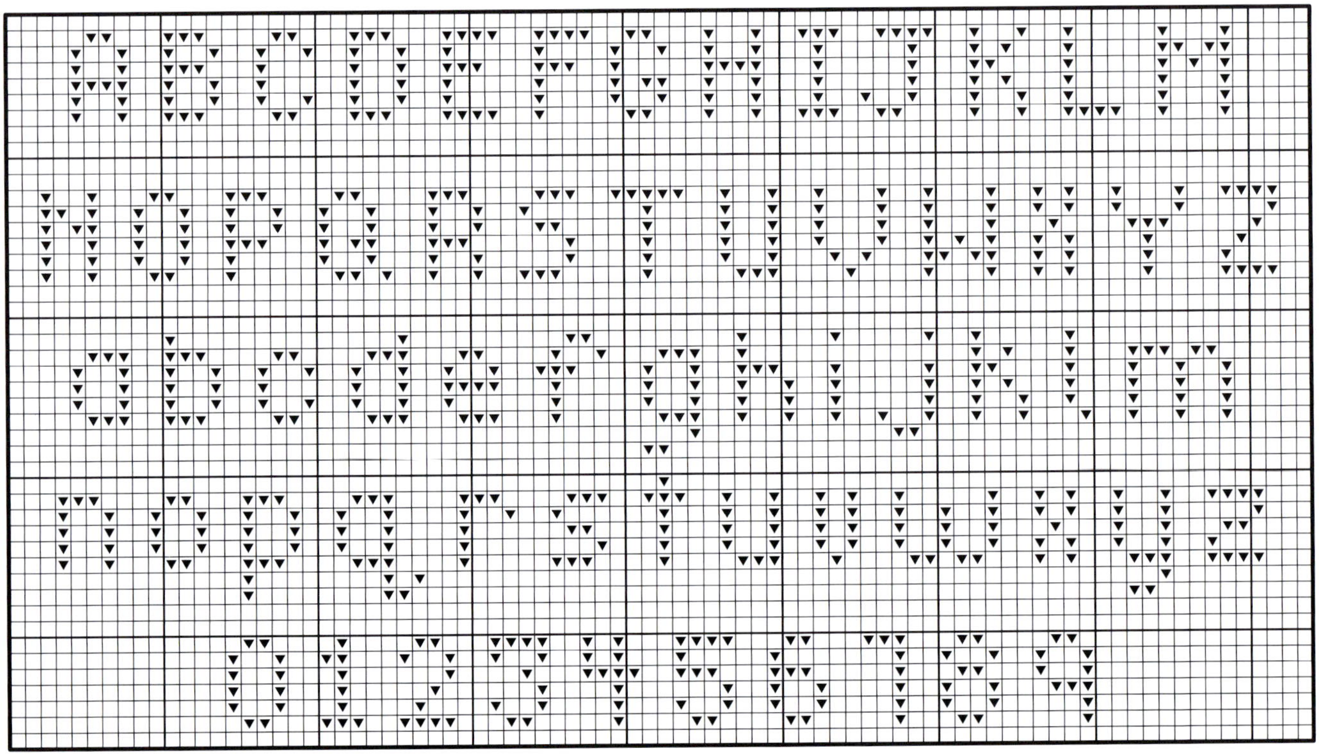

GENERAL INSTRUCTIONS

WORKING WITH ALPHABETS

Choosing Your Design

Working with alphabets is all about creativity. Choose what you want to say, then choose how it looks! Here are some guidelines to help in the creative process.

- **What you are going to stitch on will determine how you design your project.** If you are going to stitch a design on fabric that will be custom framed or finished in a way where final size is not crucial, you can use any alphabet you wish and make the design any size you want. If you're going to stitch on a prefinished item, such as a baby bib, or placed in a standard size frame, then the stitching area on your item may determine the alphabets available for use.

- **Mixing upper case letters with the lower case letters in an alphabet may make a more appealing design.** For example, stitch the first letter of a name with the upper case letter and the rest of the name with the lower case letters.

CHARTING YOUR DESIGN

A Word About Spacing

Spacing between letters and words depends on the alphabet you're using and personal preference. A good starting point is to try leaving one space between letters and three or four spaces between words. If that arrangement looks too spacey or too cramped, alter the spacing until you like the look of the design. Remember, equal spacing is not always the best spacing.

Don't forget that ***ascending*** letters like ***b***, ***d***, ***k***, and ***l*** and ***descending*** letters like ***g***, ***j***, and ***p*** take up a little more room between rows.

Arranging Your Design

1. Draw the outline of the letters from the chart on gridded paper, leaving several spaces between the letters. You may photocopy the grids on pages 29 and 30.
2. Cut the letters apart and arrange them on another piece of gridded paper until the spacing is appealing.
3. Tape the letters in place.

Fitting a Design to a Specific Stitching Area

If you are working on a design to fit a prefinished item, you need to make sure your design will fit.

1. Count the stitches in the width and height of your item's stitching area.
2. Draw the stitching area on a piece of gridded paper.
3. Chart your letters and arrange them inside the lines following the previous instructions.

STITCHING YOUR DESIGN

Figuring the Size to Cut Your Fabric

1. Count the squares in the width of your design.
2. Divide that number by the thread count of your fabric. This gives you the width of your design in inches when stitched on that particular count fabric.

   Examples:
   70 squares wide ÷ 14 ct. Aida = 5" wide
   70 squares wide ÷ 16 ct. Aida = $4^3/_8$" wide

3. Repeat the process to determine the height of the design.
4. When cutting the fabric, add at least 3" to each side of the design.

Using the Right Number of Floss Strands

The table below gives the recommended number of floss strands for common fabric thread counts.

Thread Count per Inch	Number of Strands for Cross Stitch	Number of Strands for Backstitch	Number of Strands for French Knot
12 or 13	3	1	2
14	2 or 3	1	1 or 2
16	2	1	1
18	2	1	1
20	1	1	1
22	1	1	1

HOW TO READ CHARTS

Each chart is made up of a key and a gridded design on which each square represents a stitch. The symbols in the key tell which floss color to use for each stitch in the chart. The following headings and symbols are given:

X — Cross Stitch
DMC — DMC color number
1/4**X** — Quarter Stitch
B'ST — Backstitch
COLOR — The name given to the floss color in this chart

✦ A square filled with a symbol should be worked as a **Cross Stitch**.

A small symbol in one corner of a square should be worked as a **Quarter Stitch**.

A straight line should be worked as a **Backstitch**.

A large dot listed near the end of the key should be worked as a **French Knot**.

HOW TO STITCH

*Always work **Cross Stitches** and **Quarter Stitches** first; then add the **Backstitch** and **French Knots**. When stitching, bring the threaded needle up at **1** and all **odd** numbers and down at **2** and all **even** numbers.*

Cross Stitch (X): For horizontal rows, work stitches in two journeys *(Fig. 1)*. For vertical rows, complete each stitch as shown *(Fig. 2)*.

Fig. 1

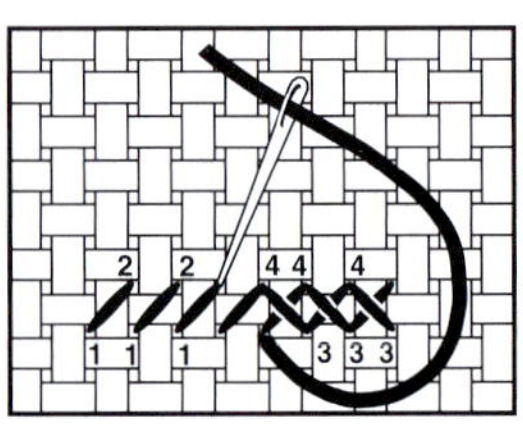

Fig. 2

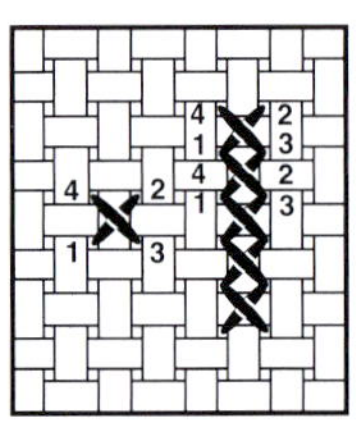

Quarter Stitch (1/4X): Come up at 1, and then split the fabric thread to go down at 2 *(Fig. 3)*.

Fig. 3

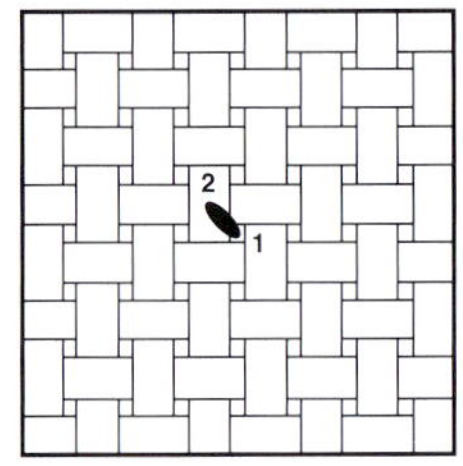

Backstitch (B'ST): For outlines and details, Backstitch should be worked after the design has been completed *(Fig. 4)*.

Fig. 4

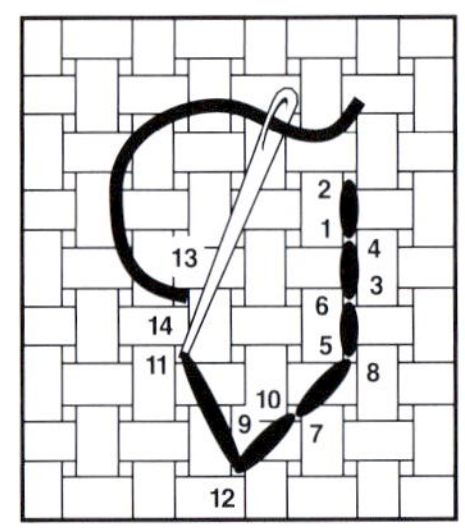

French Knot: Bring the needle up at 1. Wrap the floss once around the needle. Insert the needle at 2, tighten the knot, and pull the needle through the fabric, holding the floss until it must be released *(Fig. 5)*. For a larger knot, use more floss strands and wrap only once.

Fig. 5

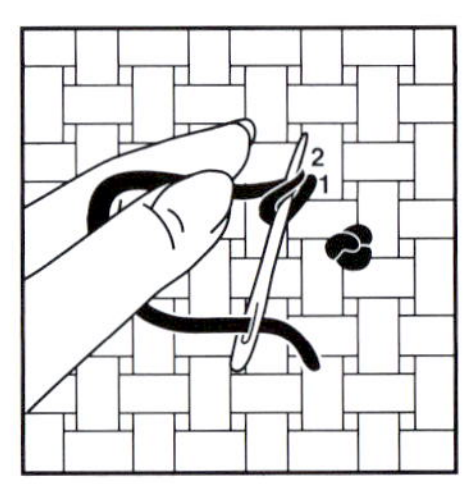

Instructions tested and photography models made by Pam Essary, Donna L. Overman, and Anne Simpson.

Production Team: Technical Writer – Mary Sullivan Hutcheson; Technical Associate – Jean Lewis; Editorial Writer – Susan Frantz Wiles; Senior Graphic Artist – Lora Puls; Graphic Artists – Frances Huddleston and Victoria Temple; Photostylist – Lori Wenger; Photographer – Jason Masters.